A LOOK AT ANCIENT CIVILIZATIONS

ANCIENT
MESOPOTAMIA

BY DANIEL R. FAUST

Gareth Stevens
PUBLISHING

CRASHCOURSE

Please visit our website, www.garethstevens.com. For a free color catalog of all our high-quality books, call toll free 1-800-542-2595 or fax 1-877-542-2596.

Cataloging-in-Publication Data

Names: Faust, Daniel R.
Title: Ancient Mesopotamia / Daniel R. Faust.
Description: New York : Gareth Stevens Publishing, 2019. | Series: A look at ancient civilizations | Includes glossary and index.
Identifiers: ISBN 9781538231555 (pbk.) | ISBN 9781538230077 (library bound) | ISBN 9781538233269 (6 pack)
Subjects: LCSH: Iraq--Civilization--To 634--Juvenile literature. | Iraq--Antiquities--Juvenile literature.
Classification: LCC DS71.F38 2019 | DDC 935--dc23

First Edition

Published in 2019 by
Gareth Stevens Publishing
111 East 14th Street, Suite 349
New York, NY 10003

Designer: Reann Nye
Editor: Tayler Cole

Photo credits: Series art (writing background) mcherevan/Shutterstock.com, (map) Andrey_Kuzmin/Shutterstock.com; cover, p. 1 muratart/Shutterstock.com; p. 5 dikobraziy/ Shutterstock.com; p. 7 Martchan/Shutterstock.com; pp. 9, 17 DEA PICTURE LIBRARY/ De Agostini/Getty Images; p. 11 HansFree/Shutterstock.com; p. 13 Veronique de Viguerie/ Getty Images News/Getty Images; p. 15 Courtesy of the Metropolitan Museum of Art; p. 19 rasoul ali/Moment Open/Getty Images; pp. 21, 25 DEA/G. DAGLI ORTI/De Agostini/Getty Images; p. 23 Sthaporn Kamlanghan/Shutterstock.com; p. 27 rasoulali/Shutterstock.com; p. 29 gokind/Shutterstock.com.

Printed in the United States of America

CPSIA compliance information: Batch #CW19GS: For further information contact Gareth Stevens, New York, New York at 1-800-542-2595.

CONTENTS

Words in the glossary appear in **bold** type the first time they are used in the text.

BETWEEN TWO RIVERS

Ancient Mesopotamia is the world's oldest civilization. Thousands of years ago, people settled between the Tigris and Euphrates Rivers in southwestern Asia. This area includes parts of the modern countries of Turkey, Syria, Iraq, and Kuwait. Mesopotamia means "between rivers" in Greek.

Black
Sea

Caspian
Sea

MESOPOTAMIA

Mediterranean
Sea

Tigris River

Euphrates River

Red
Sea

Make The Grade

Mesopotamia was part of the "fertile crescent." This was a crescent, or moon-shaped, area of land that was fertile, or great for growing crops. The world's first civilizations began in this area. It's shown in orange in the map above.

THE FIRST CIVILIZATION

Around 5000 BC, a group of people called the Sumerians moved into southeast Mesopotamia and began farming. They built **irrigation** systems to bring water to their crops. A system of government **developed** to help people work together on these big projects.

Make The Grade

Early Mesopotamian farmers may have invented a type of **plow**. These basic tools helped them grow a lot of crops but were nothing like the plows we have today.

One of the most important Sumerian inventions was the wheel! Wheels were first used to make pottery and were later used for **transportation**. The Sumerians also invented the sailboat, which helped them move goods and people along the Tigris and Euphrates Rivers.

Make The Grade

The Sumerians also created the first calendar system.
It was based on the phases of the moon.

Sumerian cities became important centers for trade. The people traded cloth, tools, and the extra grain they grew. To keep track of their traded goods, the Sumerians created a writing system called cuneiform that used about 600 **wedge**-shaped **symbols**. These symbols were pressed into soft clay tablets.

cuneiform

Make The Grade

The Sumerians also created a system of mathematics based on the number 60. This allowed them to record information about their crops and trade goods.

THE RISE OF CITY-STATES

By 3500 BC, early cities had begun to develop. At the center of each city was a building called a ziggurat that was both a **temple** and a city hall. Early cities were ruled by priests. Cities eventually became city-states ruled by kings.

ziggurat

Make The Grade

A city-state was a city that controlled nearby farms and villages. Each city-state was independent, which means it ruled itself. The Sumerian city-states were often at war with each other between 3000 and 2000 BC.

SOCIETY AND RELIGION

As Sumerian society grew,
social classes developed. In
the upper class were kings,
priests, government officials,
landowners, and rich traders.
Most Sumerians, including
farmers and skilled workers,
were in the middle class.
Slaves were the lowest class.

Make The Grade

The Sumerians had a polytheistic **religion**, which means they believed in more than one god. Their gods were like humans in many ways but were also all-powerful and could live forever.

THE AKKADIANS

The Akkadians lived in a city-state north of the Sumerians. Around 2350 BC, the Akkadians **conquered** the Sumerians and created the first ever **empire**. The Akkadian Empire strengthened its army, built roads to connect its cities, and created the first system for sending mail.

Make The Grade

King Sargon was the first Akkadian ruler. He made the city of Akkad the capital of the empire. Historians still aren't sure exactly where this city was.

THE BABYLONIANS

After about 200 years, the Akkadian Empire fell. A group called the Amorites conquered Mesopotamia around 1900 BC and picked the city of Babylon as their capital. The new empire was called Babylonia. Starting in 1792 BC, it was ruled by King Hammurabi.

Make The Grade

Hammurabi grew the Babylonian Empire by conquering cities in northern and southern Mesopotamia. Under his rule, Babylon became a very powerful city.

THE CODE OF HAMMURABI

To bring together the different groups of people of the Babylonian Empire, Hammurabi created laws for everyone to follow. The Code of Hammurabi was the first set of written laws. It was made up of 282 laws that dealt with everything from family and crime to business.

Make The Grade

The Code of Hammurabi had different **punishments** for
men and women, and for the rich and the poor. The saying
"an eye for an eye" comes from the Code of Hammurabi.

THE ASSYRIAN EMPIRE

The Assyrians were a group of people who lived in northern Mesopotamia. They had been ruled by the Babylonians for many years. The two groups had **cultures** and languages that were very alike. In the 1300s BC, the Assyrians rose to power and began to make their empire larger.

Make The Grade

The Assyrian Empire was known for its powerful army. Assyrian soldiers fought with advanced weapons including iron swords and chariots. Chariots are two-wheeled wagons pulled by horses.

By 671 BC, the Assyrians had conquered all of Mesopotamia and much of the Middle East. The Medes and the Chaldeans, two groups that were enemies of the Assyrians, decided to work together to conquer the Assyrian Empire, which fell in 609 BC.

Make The Grade

Ashurbanipal, one of the last Assyrian kings, built a famous library in the city of Nineveh. He collected thousands of cuneiform tablets created by the Sumerians and Babylonians. These works have helped historians learn about ancient Mesopotamia.

RISE OF THE PERSIAN EMPIRE

The Chaldeans and their ruler, Nebuchadnezzar II, rebuilt the city of Babylon and made it the capital of their new empire. In 539 BC, the Persian Empire conquered Babylon and then the rest of Mesopotamia. It would soon become the largest empire of its time.

Make The Grade

The Chaldean Empire is sometimes also called the
New Babylonian Empire. This was a time of great
wealth and power in Babylon, and the beautiful city
became a center for science.

ALEXANDER THE GREAT

In 331 BC, Alexander the Great conquered the Persian Empire and took control of the Mesopotamian area. By this time, however, few great Mesopotamian cities remained. Much of the culture of ancient Mesopotamia had also been lost.

Make The Grade

When Alexander conquered the Persian Empire, he mixed the Persian culture with Greek culture. By the time the Roman Empire took control, the Mesopotamian culture was almost completely gone.

TIMELINE OF ANCIENT MESOPOTAMIA

c. 5000 BC
The Sumerians move into Mesopotamia and begin farming.

c. 3500 BC
Cities ruled by priests begin to develop in Mesopotamia.

c. 2350 BC
The Akkadians conquer the Sumerians. The Akkadian Empire rises.

c. 1900 BC
The Amorites chose Babylon as their capital. The Babylonian Empire rises.

1792 BC
Hammurabi becomes king of Babylon.

1300s BC
The Assyrians rise to power.

671 BC
The Assyrians control all of Mesopotamia and much of the Middle East.

539 BC
The Persian Empire conquers Babylon.

331 BC
Alexander the Great conquers the Persian Empire.

GLOSSARY

conquer: to take by force

culture: the beliefs and ways of life of a group of people

develop: to grow and change

empire: a large area of land under the control of a single ruler

irrigation: the watering of a dry area by man-made means in order to grow plants

plow: a farm tool that is used to dig into and turn over soil

punishment: the act of making someone suffer or pay when they break a rule or law

religion: a belief in and way of honoring a god or gods

symbol: a picture, shape, or object that stands for something else

temple: a building in which people honor a god or gods

transportation: a way of traveling from one place to another

wealth: the value of all the money, land, and belongings that someone or something has

wedge: something that is shaped like a triangle

FOR MORE INFORMATION

BOOKS

Randolph, Joanne. *Living and Working in Ancient Mesopotamia*. New York, NY: Enslow Publishing, 2018.

Wood, Alix. *Uncovering the Culture of Ancient Mesopotamia*. New York, NY: Rosen Publishing Group, 2016.

WEBSITE

Mesopotamia
www.dkfindout.com/us/history/mesopotamia/
Visit this website to learn more about ancient Mesopotamia.

Publisher's note to educators and parents: Our editors have carefully reviewed this website to ensure that it is suitable for students. Many websites change frequently, however, and we cannot guarantee that a site's future contents will continue to meet our high standards of quality and educational value. Be advised that students should be closely supervised whenever they access the internet.

INDEX